FOOD LOVERS

CURRY

RECIPES SELECTED BY MARIKA KUCEROVA

Trans
Atlantic
Press

All recipes serve four people, unless otherwise indicated.

For best results when cooking the recipes in this book, buy fresh ingredients and follow the instructions carefully. Make sure that everything is properly cooked through before serving, particularly any meat and shellfish, and note that as a general rule vulnerable groups such as the very young, elderly people, pregnant women, convalescents and anyone suffering from an illness should avoid dishes that contain raw or lightly cooked eggs.

For all recipes, quantities are given in standard U.S. cups and imperial measures, followed by the metric equivalent. Follow one set or the other, but not a mixture of both because conversions may not be exact. Standard spoon and cup measurements are level and are based on the following:

1 tsp. = 5 ml, 1 tbsp. = 15 ml, 1 cup = 250 ml / 8 fl oz.

Note that Australian standard tablespoons are 20 ml, so Australian readers should use 3 tsp. in place of 1 tbsp. when measuring small quantities.

The electric oven temperatures in this book are given for conventional ovens with top and bottom heat. When using a fan oven, the temperature should be decreased by about 20–40ºF / 10–20ºC – check the oven manufacturer's instruction book for further guidance. The cooking times given should be used as an approximate guideline only.

CONTENTS

CHICKEN CURRY with TOMATOES ... 4

CHICKEN KORMA ... 6

TANDOORI FISH MASALA ... 8

VEGETABLE CURRY ... 10

GREEN CHICKEN CURRY ... 12

CHICKEN JALFREZI ... 14

LAMB ROGAN JOSH ... 16

FISH CURRY with SHRIMP ... 18

POTATO CURRY with ZUCCHINI and CASHEW NUTS ... 20

PORK CURRY with FRESH HERBS ... 22

SOUR CHICKEN CURRY ... 24

RED CHICKEN CURRY ... 26

RED BEEF CURRY ... 28

BEEF CURRY with POTATOES and NUTS ... 30

MONKFISH and GREEN COCONUT CURRY SAUCE ... 32

LAMB and SPINACH CURRY ... 34

LENTIL CURRY with PANEER ... 36

CHICKEN TIKKA MASALA ... 38

LAMB BIRYANI ... 40

TANDOORI CHICKEN KEBABS with RAITA ... 42

SHRIMP and PUMPKIN CURRY ... 44

LAMB with YOGURT SAUCE ... 46

CHICKEN CURRY
WITH TOMATOES

Ingredients

3–4 chicken breast fillets
(1 lb 6 oz/600 g)

2 tbsp. sesame oil

2 cloves garlic, chopped

1 tsp. freshly chopped ginger

Scant 1 cup/200 ml unsweetened
coconut milk

1 tbsp. tomato paste (tomato purée)

2 tsp. red curry paste

Scant ½ cup/100 ml vegetable broth
(stock)

1 lb 2 oz/500 g tomatoes

Juice of ½ lemon

2 sprigs Thai basil, shredded

2 sprigs cilantro (coriander), shredded

Salt & freshly milled pepper

Method
Prep and cook time: 30 min

1 Cut the chicken breast fillets into strips
approximately ½–¾ inches (1.5–2 cm) wide.

2 Heat the sesame oil in a wok or skillet and fry the
chicken, garlic and ginger for 3–4 minutes.

3 Then stir in the coconut milk, tomato paste
(tomato purée), curry paste and vegetable broth
(stock) and simmer for a further 4 minutes or so.

4 Drop the tomatoes into boiling water for a few
seconds, refresh in cold water, then skin, quarter,
deseed and cut into wedges. Add to the chicken
curry shortly before the end of cooking time.

5 To serve, stir the basil and cilantro (coriander)
leaves into the curry, season with salt and pepper
and add lemon juice to taste. Serve in bowls
accompanied by rice.

CHICKEN KORMA

Ingredients

1 lb 2 oz/500 g chicken breast fillet

1 sachet saffron

Good ¾ cup/200 g plain yogurt

For the spice mixture:

2 onions

3 cloves garlic

2 red chilies

1 tsp. freshly grated ginger

½ cup/50 g ground almonds

In addition:

2 tbsp. ghee or clarified butter

A good pinch of ground cardamom

½ tsp. ground cinnamon

1½ tsp. ground cumin

1½ tsp. ground coriander

1–2 lime leaves

2 curry leaves

1¾ cups/400 ml unsweetened coconut milk

Salt

Sugar

2 tbsp. chopped almonds

Chopped celery, to garnish

Method

Prep and cook time: 1 hour 15 mins
plus 4 hours to marinate

1 Cut the chicken into bite-size pieces. Dissolve the saffron in 1 tablespoon hot water and mix with the yogurt. Add the chicken pieces and marinate for about 4 hours.

2 Peel and finely chop the onions and garlic. Trim the chilies, removing the seeds if you wish, and cut into rings. Mix together the onions, garlic, chili, grated ginger and ground almonds.

3 Melt the ghee or clarified butter in a pan, add the cardamom, cinnamon, cumin and coriander and sauté briefly. Then add the prepared onion and spice mixture, the lime leaves and curry leaves and sauté, stirring, for 2–3 minutes. Now add the coconut milk and the meat with the marinade and cook for about 45 minutes. Season with salt and sugar, stir in the chopped almonds and spoon into bowls.

4 Serve sprinkled with chopped celery.

TANDOORI FISH MASALA

Ingredients

4 fish fillets, e.g. sea bream, cod, each weighing 7 oz/200 g

Salt

2 tbsp. lemon juice

2 tbsp. ghee or clarified butter, melted

For the marinade:

2 cups/400 g yogurt

3 tbsp. vinegar

1 large onion, finely chopped

3–5 cloves garlic, crushed, according to taste

½ tsp. freshly grated ginger

½–1 tsp. curcuma (turmeric)

1 pinch salt

1 pinch ground coriander

1 pinch garam masala

1 pinch chili powder

Pepper, according to taste

For the garnish:

½ red chili

1 tbsp. scallion (spring onion) rings

1 tbsp. lime zest

Method

Prep and cook time: 40 min
plus 2 hours to marinate

1 Rub the fish fillets with salt and drizzle lemon juice over the top. Place the fish in a baking dish, greased with ghee or clarified butter.

2 For the marinade, mix all the ingredients together with 1–2 tablespoons water. Pour over the fish and place in the refrigerator for 2 hours. Turn the fish from time to time.

3 Pre-heat the oven to 350°F/180°C/gas mark 4. Put the fish in the oven and cook for about 15–20 minutes. Add a little water if needed. Before serving, place the fish under a pre-heated broiler (grill) for a few minutes to brown (according to taste).

4 Divide between 4 bowls, placing a fish fillet in the center of each bowl. Cut the chili into rings and de-seed. Scatter a few chili and scallion (spring onion) rings over the fish and sprinkle some lime zest on the top. Serve hot with rice.

VEGETABLE CURRY

Ingredients

3 cups/600 g broccoli

2 cups/300 g green beans

4 carrots

1 red bell pepper

2 cloves garlic

Oil

1–2 tbsp. yellow curry paste, from an Asian grocery store

1 can coconut milk

Chili, according to taste

Salt

Cilantro (coriander) sprigs

Method

Prep and cook time: 35 min

1 Chop the broccoli into florets. Trim the beans. Peel the carrots; cut into quarters lengthways, then into pieces. Halve and de-seed the bell pepper and cut into strips. Peel the garlic and finely chop. Blanch the beans for 8 minutes in boiling, salted water, the carrots for 5 minutes and the broccoli florets for 4 minutes.

2 Drain the vegetables well.

3 Heat the curry paste with 1 tablespoon of oil in a skillet. Sauté the garlic, then pour in the coconut milk. Bring to a boil, then reduce the heat and add the bell pepper. Simmer for about 3 minutes.

4 Add the broccoli, green beans and carrots and simmer for a further 2–3 minutes. Season to taste with chili and salt.

5 Garnish the vegetable curry with fresh cilantro (coriander) sprigs and serve with rice.

GREEN CHICKEN CURRY

Ingredients

4 chicken breasts

Oil

1¾ cups/400 ml unsweetened coconut milk

2 tbsp pistachios, chopped

2 kaffir lime leaves

1 red chili pepper, deseeded and thinly sliced

½ bunch cup cilantro (coriander) leaves

For the green curry paste:

1 bunch scallions (spring onions), trimmed

3 medium-size green chilies, de-seeded and roughly chopped

2 cloves garlic, peeled

2 tsp. freshly chopped ginger

2 tsp. coriander seeds, crushed

Salt & freshly milled pepper

2 stalks lemongrass, peeled and finely chopped

½ bunch basil

1 bunch cilantro (coriander) leaves

3 tbsp. olive oil

2 untreated lemons, zest and juice

Method

Prep and cook time: 40 min plus
30 min to marinate

1 Place all ingredients for the green curry paste in a blender and process to a coarse paste.

2 Cut the chicken breasts into large pieces, mix well with about 2 tbsp of the curry paste and marinate for about 30 minutes.

3 Heat the oil in a skillet and brown the meat on all sides for about 4 minutes.

4 Stir in the remaining curry paste, cook for 2 minutes then pour in the coconut milk.

5 Add the pistachios, the kaffir lime leaves, red chili pepper and cilantro (coriander) leaves. Bring to a boil, then simmer gently for about 25 minutes. Season to taste with salt and serve with the rice.

CHICKEN JALFREZI

Ingredients

1 lb 2 oz/500 g chicken breast fillets

1 tbsp. Worcestershire sauce

3 onions

7 oz/200 g sugarsnap peas

1 cup/150 g frozen peas

2 red chilies, or more according
to taste

3 tbsp. oil

A good pinch of brown mustard seeds

A good pinch of cumin seeds

A good pinch of ground cumin

A pinch of ground coriander

A good pinch of ground turmeric

2/3–3/4 cup/150–200 ml coconut
cream, to taste

Salt & freshly milled pepper

Mint leaves

Method
Prep and cook time: 25 min

1 Cut the meat into thin strips and mix with the Worcestershire sauce. Peel, halve and slice the onions. Trim the sugarsnap peas. Thaw the frozen peas. Slit the chilies open lengthways, remove the seeds and inner ribs, and finely chop the flesh.

2 Heat the oil in a skillet and fry the mustard seeds and cumin seeds, stirring, for about 30 seconds, until they start to pop. Add the onions and chilies and fry, stirring, until the onions are lightly browned.

3 Stir in the meat, ground spices, Worcestershire sauce, sugarsnap peas and thawed frozen peas and season with salt and pepper. Add 1 cup of water, bring to a boil and cook over a medium heat for a further 3–5 minutes, stirring, until the meat and vegetables are just cooked.

4 Add coconut cream to taste. Sprinkle with mint and serve with rice.

LAMB ROGAN JOSH

Ingredients

6 cloves garlic

1 tsp freshly grated ginger

6 tbsp. oil

8 cardamom seeds

1 inch/2.5 cm cinnamon stick

2 bay leaves

1 lb 12 oz/800 g lamb, from the leg, cut into bite-size pieces

2 onions, chopped

1–2 tsp. cumin

1–2 tsp. ground coriander

½ tsp. cayenne pepper, according to taste

1 tbsp. sweet paprika

1–2 tbsp. tomato paste (purée)

Salt

Method

Prep and cook time: 1 hour 20 min

1 Peel the garlic and crush in a garlic press. Mix the garlic with the freshly grated ginger.

2 Heat the oil in a large skillet. Fry the cardamom, cinnamon and bay leaves in the oil, then add the meat and fry until browned on all sides.

3 Take the meat out of the skillet and fry the onions, then add the garlic–ginger mixture. Now add the cumin, coriander, cayenne pepper, paprika and tomato paste (purée) and stir. Add the meat, season to taste with salt and pour in 1¼ cups /300 ml water.

4 Bring to a boil and simmer gently for about 1 hour. Serve with rice.

FISH CURRY
WITH *SHRIMP*

Ingredients

2 onions

4 cloves garlic

1 tsp. curcuma (turmeric)

2 tsp. curry powder

1 lb/450 g haddock, cut into bite-size pieces, skin and bones removed

4 tbsp. ghee or clarified butter

2 tsp. freshly grated ginger

1 tsp. mustard seeds

5 oz/150 g canned tomatoes

½ tsp. finely chopped red chili

1¾ cups/400 ml unsweetened coconut milk

6 oz/175 g large shrimp or prawns, peeled and ready to cook

Vegetable broth (stock)

1 tbsp. finely chopped cilantro (coriander)

Method
Prep and cook time: 35 min

1 Peel and finely chop the onions and garlic. Mix the curcuma (turmeric) and curry powder and rub the fish with about half of the mixture. Reserve the remainder.

2 Heat the ghee or clarified butter in a large skillet and sauté the onions and garlic until translucent. Then add the ginger, the remaining spice mix and mustard seeds and fry briefly. Then add the tomatoes and coconut milk and simmer for about 10 minutes. Purée the sauce, but not too finely.

3 Add the chopped chili, fish and shrimp (or prawns) and cook gently for about 5 minutes, until done. If the sauce is too thick, add a little vegetable broth (stock).

4 Check the seasoning and serve garnished with cilantro (coriander).

POTATO CURRY WITH ZUCCHINI AND CASHEW NUTS

Ingredients

3 cups/500 g small zucchini (courgettes)

1½ cups/300 g tomatoes

2¼ lb/1 kg boiling potatoes

1 red onion

1 clove garlic

1 oz/25 g ginger

2 tbsp. ghee or clarified butter

1 tbsp. curry powder, according to taste

1 tsp. ground cumin

Salt & freshly milled pepper

2 cups/500 ml vegetable broth (stock)

1 tbsp. potato starch

½ cup/60 g cashew nuts, roasted

Method

Prep and cook time: 45 min

1 Trim the zucchini (courgettes) and cut into cubes. Cut the tomatoes into quarters and de-seed. Peel the potatoes and dice. Blanch the potatoes in boiling salted water for 8 minutes, then drain. Peel the onion and the garlic and chop. Peel the ginger and finely chop.

2 Fry the potatoes in hot ghee or clarified butter. Add the zucchini and sauté, then stir in the garlic, onion and ginger and fry. Season with curry powder, cumin, salt and pepper. Now add the tomatoes and pour in the vegetable broth (stock). Simmer for 15–20 minutes.

3 Mix the potato starch to a paste with a drop of cold water, then stir the mixture into the hot curry. Bring to a boil, then simmer and season to taste.

4 Sprinkle a few roasted cashew nuts over the top and serve on warmed plates.

PORK CURRY
WITH FRESH HERBS

Ingredients

1½ lb/700 g lean pork (without skin or bones)

1 onion

1 dried chili

3 tbsp. oil

2 tsp. finely grated fresh ginger

A good pinch of ground coriander

½ tsp. ground curcuma (turmeric)

A good pinch of ground cumin

A pinch of ground cloves

2 tbsp. dark soy sauce

Salt & freshly milled pepper

1 tbsp. chopped parsley

Scallion greens, cut into rings

Method

Prep and cook time: 1 hour

1 Roughly dice the meat. Peel and dice the onion. Chop the dried chili.

2 Heat the oil and quickly brown the meat on all sides. Season with salt and pepper and add the onion, ginger and chili. Fry gently for about 3 minutes. Then stir in the coriander, curcuma (turmeric), cumin and cloves, and add ¾–1 cup/ 200 ml water and the soy sauce. Cover and cook for about 45 minutes.

3 Serve sprinkled with parsley and scallion rings.

SOUR CHICKEN CURRY

Ingredients

2 chicken breasts (1 lb 2 oz/500 g)

2 tbsp. soy sauce

1 cup/200 g rice

Curry powder (1 good pinch of each of the following ground spices: coriander, black pepper, ginger, paprika, nutmeg, mustard seed, cloves, cardamom, fenugreek, cumin)

1 pinch each of curcuma (turmeric), chili powder, cinnamon

1 onion

2 green bell peppers

7 oz/200 g snow peas (mangetout)

1 red chili

1 tbsp. sesame oil

Scant ½ cup/100 ml vegetable broth (stock)

2 tbsp. lemon juice

Salt

Method

Prep and cook time: 45 min

1 Preheat the oven to 325°F/160°C/gas mark 3. Cut the chicken breast into thin strips and sprinkle with soy sauce.

2 Wash the rice in a sieve under running water, then put into a pan with just double the amount of lightly salted water and bring to a boil. Cover and cook over a very low heat for about 20 minutes

3 Mix the curcuma (turmeric), chili powder and cinnamon. Sprinkle them over the meat and knead into it.

4 Peel and finely dice the onion. Trim, halve and core the bell peppers and cut the flesh into very thin strips. Slice the snow peas (mangetout) into long strips. Slit open the chili lengthways and remove the seeds and the white inner ribs. Cut the flesh into very thin strips.

5 Heat the oil in a nonstick skillet and sauté the chicken on all sides, until it is cooked through. Take out of the skillet, put on a plate, cover with aluminum foil and keep warm in the preheated oven.

6 Put the prepared vegetables into the skillet and fry lightly. Add the vegetable broth (stock) and curry powder, to taste, and simmer for 3–5 minutes. Season with salt and pepper and add lemon juice to taste. Add the cooked rice to the vegetables and mix well.

7 Spoon into bowls. Put the chicken on top of the vegetable rice and serve hot.

RED CHICKEN CURRY

Ingredients

1 lb 6 oz/600 g chicken breasts

3 tomatoes

1 cup/200 g pineapple pieces

2 stalks lemongrass

1 tbsp. oil

1¾ cups/400 ml unsweetened coconut milk

1 tbsp. brown sugar

3 tbsp. fish sauce

2 tbsp. lime juice

kaffir lime leaves, for garnish

For the red curry paste:

About 1 inch/2.5 cm galangal

1 shallot, peeled

1 clove garlic, peeled

About 1 inch/2.5 cm lemongrass

2 Thai chilies

Zest of a kaffir lime

½–1 tsp. shrimp paste

Salt

Method
Prep and cook time: 30 min

1 For the red curry paste place all the ingredients except for the shrimp paste and the salt in a mortar and finely crush. Now mix in the salt and the shrimp paste and stir until smooth.

2 Cut the chicken breasts into 1 inch (2.5 cm) pieces. Place the tomatoes into boiling water, then immediately into cold water. Peel, quarter, de-seed and chop the tomatoes. Chop the pineapple into small pieces. Trim the lemongrass, then finely chop.

3 Heat the oil in a wok or skillet. Fry the curry paste, then pour in the coconut milk and bring to a boil. Season with lemongrass, sugar, fish sauce and lime juice. Add the chicken pieces and the pineapple and simmer for about 5 minutes. Now add the tomatoes and heat until cooked.

4 Divide into 4 bowls and serve.

RED BEEF CURRY

Ingredients

1 lb 6 oz/600 g beef, e. g. rump

14 oz/400 g sweet potatoes

2 red bell peppers

1½ cups/250 g string beans

1 onion

2 cloves garlic

1–2 tsp. shrimp paste

½ tsp. chili flakes

1 tsp. ginger, freshly grated

3 tbsp. oil

9 fl oz/250 ml coconut milk

2 kaffir lime leaves

Salt

Light soy sauce

Method

Prep and cook time: 50 min

1 Cut the beef into strips.

2 Peel the sweet potatoes and roughly chop.

3 Halve, de-seed and cut the bell peppers into strips. Trim the string beans.

4 Peel the onion and the garlic and finely chop.

5 Fry the shrimp paste, chili, ginger, onion and garlic in hot oil. Add the meat and fry, then pour in the coconut milk. Add a little water and the vegetables. Throw in the lime leaves and simmer gently for about 30 minutes, stirring occasionally. Add a little water if needed. Season with salt and soy sauce and serve.

BEEF CURRY
WITH POTATOES AND NUTS

Ingredients

1 lb 6 oz/600 g beef

2 shallots

2 cloves garlic

3 tbsp. sesame oil

2 red chilies: dried

½ cup/50 g peanuts, fresh, not salted

3 cups/800 ml coconut cream

14 oz/400 g boiling potatoes

4 tbsp. fish sauce

1 tbsp. oyster sauce

2 tbsp. brown sugar

2 tbsp. lime juice

4 slices of lime, fried

For the curry paste:

1 shallot

2 cloves garlic

4 cm galangal

2 red chilies

1 tsp. shrimp paste

Salt

Method

Prep and cook time: 1 hour 30 min

1 For the curry paste, peel the shallot and the garlic and crush in a mortar together with the galangal and chili until smooth or process in a blender. Stir in the shrimp paste and salt to taste.

2 Cut the beef into thin strips.

3 Peel the shallots and the garlic and finely chop. Heat 1 tablespoon of the oil in a wok and fry the shallots, the garlic and the chilies over a high heat until the shallots are golden brown. Take out of the wok. Let cool slightly, then place in the mortar and crush to a smooth paste.

4 Put the peanuts in the wok and toast until golden brown.

5 Place in a clean mortar and crush. Fry the meat in the remaining oil over a high heat and pour in half of the coconut cream. Bring to a boil, then reduce the heat and simmer for 45 minutes.

6 In the meantime peel the potatoes and cut into about 1 inch (3 cm) cubes. Take the meat and the sauce out of the wok and clean the wok.

7 Sauté the curry paste in the wok, pour in the remaining coconut cream, add the potatoes, the crushed peanuts and the shallot paste and bring to a boil. Cook for 5 minutes, then add the meat and season with fish sauce, oyster sauce and sugar. Simmer for about 25 minutes over a medium heat until the potatoes are cooked.

8 Season to taste with lime juice and spoon into bowls. Garnish with fried lime slices and serve.

MONKFISH
AND GREEN COCONUT CURRY SAUCE

Ingredients

2¼ lb/1 kg monk fish fillets

Salt

4 tbsp. lemon juice

2 tbsp. light soy sauce

4–5 scallions (spring onions), white part only

1 zucchini (courgette)

4 kaffir lime leaves

Scant 1 cup/200 ml unsweetened coconut milk

3–4 tbsp. oil

3 sprigs Thai basil

For the curry paste:

1 shallot, peeled

1 clove garlic, peeled

1 green chili

1 tbsp. cilantro (coriander) leaves

1 tsp. coriander root, chopped

1 pinch galangal, ground

4 peppercorns

½ tsp. coriander seeds

Method

Prep and cook time: 30 min plus 30 to marinate

1 For the curry paste, place all ingredients in a mortar and grind to a smooth paste.

2 Skin the fish and cut into 1 inch (2.5 cm) pieces. Marinate the fish pieces with the salt, lemon juice and soy sauce for about 30 minutes.

3 Trim the scallions (spring onions) and slice into rings. Trim the zucchini (courgette), cut in half lengthways, then thinly slice. Finely chop the kaffir lime leaves.

4 Heat the coconut milk over a low heat and simmer for 5 minutes. Heat the oil in a wok and fry the fish for about 4 minutes. Pour in the coconut milk and the curry paste and the rest of the marinade. (If you don't use all the curry paste, put the remainder in a jar and keep it in the refrigerator.) Reduce the heat and simmer the fish for 3 minutes.

5 Add the scallions, zucchini, some basil leaves and lime leaves and cook for a further 3 minutes.

6 Scoop the curry onto warmed plates and garnish with the remaining basil leaves. Serve with basmati rice.

LAMB AND SPINACH CURRY

Ingredients

2¼ lb/1 kg lamb, shoulder or leg

3 onions

2 cloves garlic

1 piece fresh ginger, 1 inch/
about 2.5 cm

2 red chilies, finely chopped

½ tsp. paprika, noble sweet

A pinch of ground cloves

1 tsp. curcuma (turmeric)

1 tsp. ground coriander

Salt

¼ cup/50 g yogurt

Scant 1 cup/about 200 ml lamb broth
(stock)

7 oz/200 g spinach

3 tbsp. oil

2 tbsp. chopped cilantro (coriander)
leaves

Method

Prep and cook time: 1 hour 45 min
plus 1 hour to marinate

1 Cut the meat into 1½ inch (4 cm) cubes. Peel the onions, halve lengthways and slice thinly. Peel the garlic and finely dice 1 clove.

2 Peel and grate the ginger. Press the remaining garlic clove into the ginger. Mix the ginger and garlic with the rest of the spices and ½ teaspoon salt, then add to the yogurt and mix well. Mix the meat with the yogurt marinade, cover and marinate in the refrigerator for about 1 hour.

3 Heat the oil in a skillet. Gently sweat the onion slices for about 3 minutes before adding the diced garlic and sautéing for a further minute. Add the meat with the marinade. Cover and simmer over a low heat for about 1¼ hours, gradually adding the lamb stock and stirring frequently.

4 Wash and roughly chop the spinach and add to the lamb during the last 15 minutes of cooking time.

5 Check the seasoning and serve with rice.

LENTIL CURRY WITH PANEER

Ingredients

2 onions

2 cloves garlic

2 tbsp. ghee or clarified butter

1 tsp. curcuma (turmeric)

Pinch of ground cloves

Pinch of ground cumin

Pinch of ground allspice

2 curry leaves

1 cup/250 ml unsweetened coconut milk

1¾ cups/about 400 ml vegetable broth (stock)

1 cup/200 g black lentils

1 cup/200 g red lentils

Salt & freshly milled pepper

7 oz/200 g paneer cheese

Method

Prep and cook time: 35 min

1 Peel and finely chop the onions and garlic. Heat the ghee (or clarified butter) and sauté the onions and garlic, add the spices and sauté briefly before pouring in the coconut milk. Stir in a little broth (stock) and the black lentils, cover and simmer gently for about 10 minutes.

2 Add the red lentils and a little more broth. Simmer for a further 10 minutes or so, stirring occasionally and add the rest of the broth as necessary.

3 Finally remove the curry leaves and season to taste with salt and pepper.

4 Dice the paneer and add to the curry. Serve with flatbread.

CHICKEN TIKKA MASALA

Ingredients

1 oven-ready chicken, 2½–3 lb /1.2–1.4 kg

1 lemon

Salt & freshly milled pepper

For the marinade:

2 tsp. freshly grated ginger

2 cloves garlic

2 cups/500 g yogurt

2 tbsp. vegetable oil

2 tbsp. paprika

Spice mixture: ½ tsp. ground cumin, black pepper, chili powder and turmeric

1 tbsp. cilantro (coriander) leaves, chopped

Method

Prep and cook time: 1 hour 15 min
plus 8 hours to marinate

1 Joint into the chicken into 6–8 pieces. Score the surface of the chicken pieces to a depth of ¼ inch (0.5 cm) and put into a shallow dish. Sprinkle with pepper, salt and the juice of a lemon. Let stand for about 30 minutes.

2 Peel the ginger and garlic. Press the garlic. Mix all the spices for the marinade with the yogurt and the oil. Coat the chicken pieces generously with the marinade and seal the dish with aluminum foil. Marinate the chicken in the refrigerator for 8 hours or overnight.

3 Preheat the oven to 350°F/180°C/gas mark 4. Line a cookie sheet with aluminum foil and put the chicken pieces on the sheet. Cook in the oven for 35–40 minutes, brushing frequently with marinade (using about a quarter), and adding a little water if necessary.

4 Heat the remaining marinade in a large pan and add the chicken pieces. Continue to heat very gently for 5 minutes, then sprinkle with cilantro (coriander) and serve with rice.

LAMB BIRYANI

Ingredients

1½ lb/650 g lamb (leg)

1–2 onions, finely chopped

7 tbsp. ghee or clarified butter

2 tsp. freshly grated ginger

3 cloves garlic, pressed

6 cardamom pods

5 cloves

1 piece cinnamon stick (¾-1 inch /2–3 cm)

½ tsp. ground cumin

½ tsp. turmeric

Chili powder, to taste

⅔ cup/150 g yogurt

⅔ cup/150 ml meat broth (stock)

Salt

1½ cups/300 g basmati rice

⅓ cup/50 g raisins

4 tbsp. milk

A few saffron threads

6 tbsp. blanched almonds

Cilantro (coriander) leaves to garnish

Method

Prep and cook time: 2h 15 min

1 Cut the meat into bite-size pieces. Heat 4 tbsp of ghee (or clarified butter) in a pan and sauté half of the onions until translucent. Add the ginger, cardamom, garlic, cloves, cinnamon and meat and fry, stirring frequently, until the meat is lightly browned on all sides. Stir in the ground spices, yogurt and broth (stock) and season with salt. Cover and simmer over a low heat for 45–60 minutes, stirring occasionally (it will be very thick).

2 Sauté the rest of the onions in a pan without letting them color. Wash the rice in a sieve under running water and add to the onions with just double the amount of lightly salted water. Bring to a boil and cook, covered, over a very low heat for about 5 minutes.

3 Put the meat into a greased baking dish. Drain the rice and mix with the raisins. Heat the milk, add the saffron and 2 tablespoons ghee and let them dissolve. Add the milk to the rice and mix with the meat in the dish.

4 Put a lid on the dish (or seal with aluminum foil) and cook in a preheated oven (350°F/180°C/gas mark 4, middle shelf) for about 1 hour.

5 Lightly toast the almonds in the remaining ghee and add to the dish.

6 Before serving fluff up the lamb biryani with a fork, season to taste and spoon onto plates. Scatter some cilantro (coriander) over the top and serve.

TANDOORI CHICKEN KEBABS
WITH RAITA

Ingredients

4 chicken breast fillets

1 lemon

Salt & freshly milled pepper

For the marinade:

2 cloves garlic

Scant 1 cup/200 g yogurt

2 tbsp. vegetable oil

2 tsp. freshly grated ginger

2 tsp. paprika

Spice mixture: 1 tsp each of ground: cumin, nutmeg, cilantro (coriander), black pepper, paprika

For the raita:

1 cucumber

1 cup/250 g yogurt

½ tsp. ground caraway

½ tsp. ground coriander

1 tbsp. finely chopped parsley

1 tbsp. finely chopped mint

Salt & freshly milled pepper

Mint, to garnish

Method

Prep and cook time: 30 min plus 8 hours to marinate

1 Cut the chicken into bite-size cubes and put into a shallow dish. Sprinkle with pepper, salt and lemon juice and let stand for about 30 minutes.

2 Peel the garlic. Mix the yogurt with the oil and the spices to make a marinade and press the garlic into it. Coat the chicken generously with the marinade and seal the dish with aluminum foil. Marinate in the refrigerator for 8 hours or overnight.

3 For the raita, peel the cucumber, halve lengthways, scrape out the seeds and grate the cucumber. Mix with the yogurt, add the caraway, coriander, parsley and mint and season with salt and pepper. Let stand for about 1 hour. Garnish with mint.

4 Thread the chicken onto skewers. Preheat a broiler (grill). Lay aluminum foil on the grill rack and put the kebabs on the foil. Grill for 8–10 minutes, brushing with marinade from time to time.

5 Serve the chicken kebabs with the raita.

SHRIMP AND PUMPKIN CURRY

Ingredients

1 bunch scallions (spring onions)

2 cloves garlic

1 lb 6 oz/600 g pumpkin

2 tsp. freshly chopped ginger

2 tbsp. oil

1¾ cups/400 ml unsweetened coconut milk

Juice of ½ lemon

Salt & pepper

11 oz/300 g frozen shrimp (prawns)

For the green curry paste:

1 shallot, roughly chopped

1 peeled garlic clove

1 tbsp. cilantro (coriander) leaves

½ tsp. coriander seeds

1 tsp. freshly grated ginger

1 green chili, deseeded and roughly chopped

Method

Prep and cook time: 30 min

1 Put all the ingredients for the curry paste into a mortar and crush to make a paste.

2 Trim the scallions (spring onions) and cut into rings. Peel and chop the garlic. Peel and deseed the pumpkin and cut into ½ inch (1 cm cubes).

3 Heat the oil and sauté the scallions, ginger, garlic and pumpkin over a high heat for 4–5 minutes. Stir in the coconut milk, curry paste and lemon juice, season with salt and pepper and simmer without a lid over a medium heat for about 5 minutes.

4 Check the seasoning, add the shrimp (prawns) and briefly return to a boil. When the shrimp are cooked, serve in bowls.

LAMB WITH YOGURT SAUCE

Ingredients

2¼ lb/1 kg lamb, e.g. shoulder

2 onions

2 cloves garlic

3 tbsp. ghee or clarified butter

1 tsp. turmeric

1 tbsp. paprika, noble sweet

Spice mixture: 1 good pinch each of ground: cumin, coriander seeds, allspice, cloves and cinnamon

1 cup/250 g yogurt

For the rice:

1¼ cups/250 g basmati rice

4 cardamom pods

4 cloves

1 cinnamon stick

2 fresh bay leaves

1 tsp. turmeric

For the yogurt sauce:

1¾ cups/400 g yogurt

Juice of 1 lemon

1 tbsp. mint, chopped

Salt

Method

Prep and cook time: 2 hours

1 Cut the meat into large cubes.

2 Peel and chop the onions and garlic.

3 Heat the ghee (or clarified butter) and brown the meat over a fairly high heat. Add the onions, garlic and spices. Deglaze with a little water and add the yogurt. Cover and cook in the oven at 350°F/180°C/gas mark 4 for about 1½ hours. Stir occasionally and add more water if necessary.

4 Wash the rice and put into a pan with the spices. Add double the amount of water, cover and bring to a boil. Simmer for about 25 minutes, until cooked.

5 For the yogurt sauce, mix all the ingredients and season to taste with salt.

6 Take the lid off the curry and let brown for about 10 minutes. Check the seasoning and serve with the rice, the yogurt sauce and poppadoms.

Published by Transatlantic Press

First published in 2010

Transatlantic Press
38 Copthorne Road, Croxley Green, Hertfordshire WD3 4AQ

© Transatlantic Press

Images and Recipes by StockFood © The Food Image Agency

Recipes selected by Marika Kucerova, StockFood

A catalogue record for this book is available from the British Library.

ISBN 978-1-908533-51-7

Printed in China